# Am... PLANTS

## by Honor Head

An Hachette UK Company
www.hachette.co.uk

First published in the USA in 2013 by TickTock, an imprint of Octopus Publishing Group Ltd
Endeavour House, 189 Shaftesbury Avenue, London, WC2H 8JY
www.octopusbooks.co.uk  www.octopusbooksusa.com
Copyright © Octopus Publishing Group Ltd 2013
Distributed in the US by Hachette Book Group, USA, 237 Park Avenue, New York, NY 10017, USA
Distributed in Canada by Canadian Manda Group, 165 Dufferin Street, Toronto, Ontario, Canada M6K 3H6

ISBN 978 1 84898 861 3

Printed and bound in China
10 9 8 7 6 5 4 3 2 1

With thanks to Marjorie Frank
Natural history consultant: Dr. Kim Dennis-Bryan F.Z.S
US Editor: Jennifer Dixon    Cover design: Steve West    Production Controller: Alexandra Bell

Picture credits (t=top; b=bottom; c=center; l=left; r=right):
Arcticphoto.co.uk: 9c. Corbis: 27. FLPA: 12b, 13, 16b, 17t, 18c, 19t, 26b, 28b, 30b, 31t. Floridanature.com: 28tl, 29t.
Nature Picture Library: 19 main. Shutterstock: OFC, 1, 2, 3, 4tl, 4c, 4b, 5tl, 5r, 5cl, 5bl, 6tl, 6l, 6r, 7cr, 7 main, 8tl, 9t, 9b, 10tl, 10
main, 11t, 11b, 12tl, 12tr, 12cr, 14, 15, 18tl, 18b, 20tl, 22tl, 22, 23, 25bl, 25br, 26tl, 30tl, OBC.
Stephen Mifsud – www.MaltaWildPlants.com: 24tl, 24b, 25t. Superstock: 7t, 16tl, 17b, 20l, 21tr, 21 main, 26c, 29b, 31b.
TickTock image archive: map page 8.

Every effort has been made to trace copyright holders, and we apologize in advance for any omissions.
We would be pleased to insert the appropriate acknowledgments in any subsequent edition of this publication.

# Contents

Words that look **bold like this** are in the glossary.

# What is a plant?

Plants are living things. Most plants grow from the ground. Many plants produce flowers, **fruits**, and **seeds**. Plants come in many different shapes and sizes. Trees and shrubs are also plants.

**We eat the fruits of an orange tree.**

Flowers are usually brightly colored.

Flowers attract birds and insects. The birds and insects pollinate flowers, which helps the plant to **reproduce**.

**Some flowers have a sweet smell that attracts insects.**

Grass is a plant that is eaten by many animals.

Wheat is a crop plant with seeds that we call grain. We cannot eat the grain raw, but we make it into flour and use it to make bread.

## Ferns

Mosses and ferns are plants that do not produce flowers.

Mosses and ferns can grow in damp places where there is not much light.

## Moss

# Parts of a plant

The majority of plants have roots, stems, and leaves. Most plants have roots that grow in the ground. The roots push down into the **soil** to hold the plant in place. Above the ground are the stem, leaves, and flowers.

This bird of paradise plant has a flower that looks like a bird!

Plants can make their own food inside themselves. The plant's leaves use sunlight to make food for the plant.

**Leaves**

The plant's stem carries food from the roots to the other parts of the plant. It also carries the leaves towards sunlight.

**Stem**

**Roots**

The plant's roots draw in water and **nutrients** from the soil to feed the plant.

The stems of some plants grow around other plants. Lianas, which grow in **rainforests**, do this.

**Tree trunk**

**Liana stem**

*A tree has a hard woody stem called a trunk.*

**Leaf**

The plants in this picture are living stone plants. They have two thick fleshy leaves that look like stones, or pebbles, on the ground.

Flowers are the most colorful parts of plants. Leaves vary from yellow through red to green.

# Plant habitats

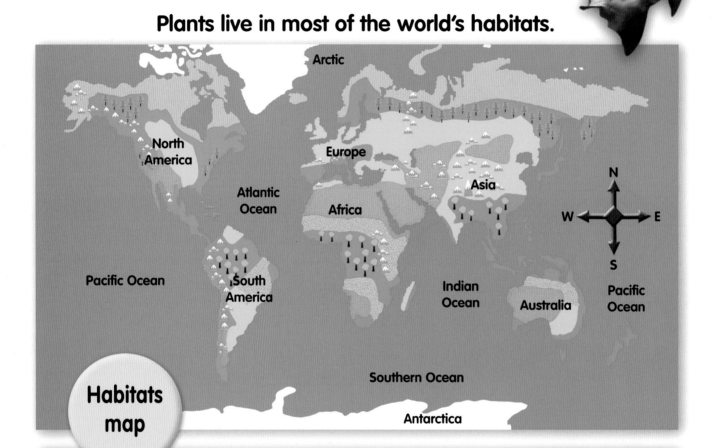

This saguaro cactus grows in deserts.

A habitat is the place where a plant or an animal lives. Plants can grow in many different habitats, including the sea! The greatest number of different plants grow in warm, wet rainforests.

## Plants live in most of the world's habitats.

Arctic

North America

Europe

Asia

Atlantic Ocean

Africa

Pacific Ocean

South America

Indian Ocean

Australia

Pacific Ocean

Southern Ocean

Antarctica

N
W — E
S

**Habitats map**

## Map key
This map key shows you what the colors and pictures on the map mean.

Temperate grasslands – areas that are dry in summer

Tropical grasslands – hot, dry areas with few trees

Tundra – cold, windy places

Cool, rainy forests

Arctic/Antarctica – frozen, snowy ground and icy seas

Cold forests

Warm, wet rainforest

Deserts – dry land with little rain

Long strands of plantlike seaweed grow in the ocean. Seaweed has no roots but has a special part called a "holdfast" to keep it in one place.

## Seaweed uses the holdfast to cling on to rocks.

On the cold, icy Arctic tundra, plants grow in clumps low to the ground, which protects them from high winds.

**Some Arctic plants have hairs on their leaves, which helps reduce water loss.**

### AMAZING PLANT FACT
The sharp prickles on a cactus are actually the plant's leaves. The prickles lose less water than normal leaves in the hot **desert** habitat.

# Seeds and bulbs

New plants can grow from a seed or a bulb.
A seed is like a small case that contains everything needed to make a new plant.

**The black dots in this kiwi fruit are the seeds.**

A bulb grows at the bottom of the plant under the ground. During the summer the plant stores food in the bulb.

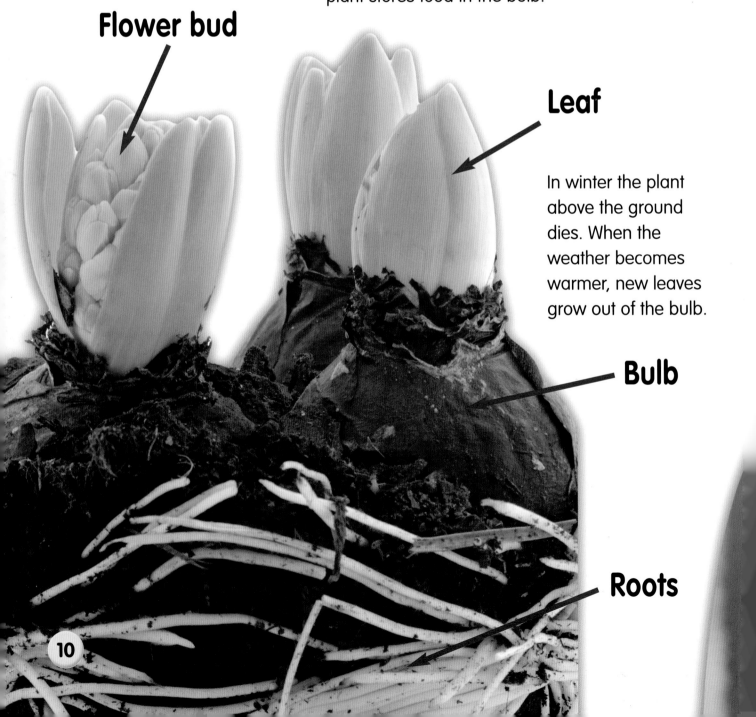

**Flower bud**

**Leaf**

In winter the plant above the ground dies. When the weather becomes warmer, new leaves grow out of the bulb.

**Bulb**

**Roots**

Most plants have flowers. The flower's anthers are covered in a fine yellow dust called **pollen**.

**Stigma**

**Anther**

In the middle of the flower are the stamens, the male parts. Each stamen has an anther at the top. The female part is called the carpel. It has a section called a stigma at the top.

Insects such as bees carry pollen from the anthers of one flower to the stigma of another flower. This is called **pollination**. After pollination, a seed is made.

**AMAZING PLANT FACT**
Insects such as bees and butterflies visit flowers to drink sweet **nectar**.

This bee is covered in pollen from the anthers of flowers it has visited.

# Scattering seeds

Plants have many ways of making sure their seeds find a way of leaving the mother plant and growing in a new place. Some plants are blown away from their mother plant by the wind.

Each dandelion seed blows to a new place to live.

Tumbleweed is a bush that breaks away from its roots in fall. The wind pushes it along the ground and it scatters its seeds as it rolls along.

**Tumbleweed**

Some animals help seeds to spread. Squirrels eat acorns. They collect them and bury them.

Inside the acorns are the seeds of the oak tree.

This macaw is eating a palm fruit.

**AMAZING PLANT FACT**

Birds eat the seeds in fruit. The seeds pass through the bird's gut and fall to the ground in their droppings. The seeds grow into new plants.

# What is a life cycle?

A life cycle is all the different **stages** and changes that a plant or animal goes through in its life. This diagram shows a plant life cycle. It is the life cycle of a sunflower.

Sunflower seeds are a tasty snack for birds and people.

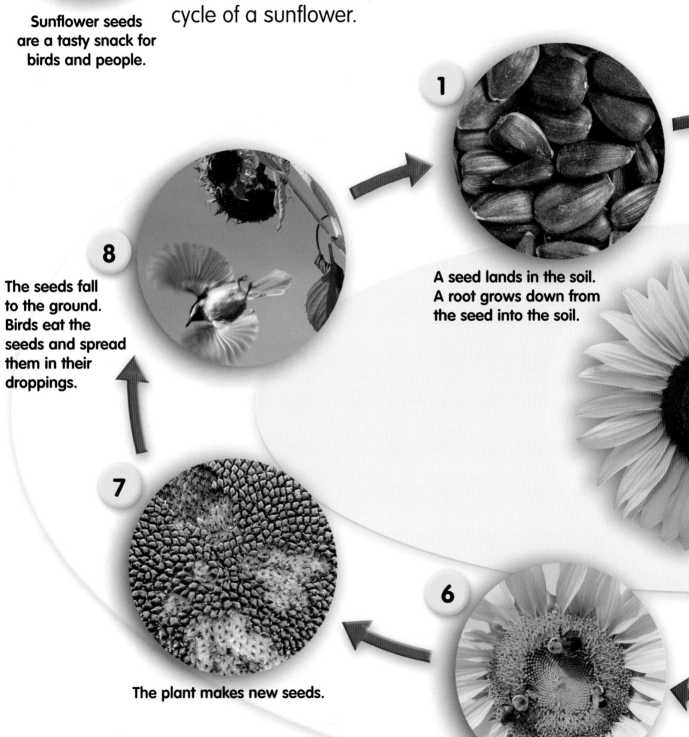

**1**

A seed lands in the soil. A root grows down from the seed into the soil.

**8**

The seeds fall to the ground. Birds eat the seeds and spread them in their droppings.

**7**

The plant makes new seeds.

**6**

Insects pollinate the flower.

# Amazing plant life cycles

A pitcher plant

In this book we are going to find out about some amazing plant life cycles – from meat-eating pitcher plants to coconut palm trees.

A coconut palm tree

**2**

A shoot starts to grow above the ground from the seed. The shoot in this picture is covered by the seed's outer coat.

**3**

Tiny leaves appear on the shoot.

**4**

The shoot grows taller and stronger. More leaves grow. The leaves get bigger.

**5**

A bud appears and grows into a flower.

# Rafflesia

Before a plant can make a seed it has to be pollinated. This is usually done by insects that land on the plant and carry the pollen to another plant.

**This is the bud of a rafflesia flower.**

## AMAZING PLANT FACT

The rafflesia is the world's biggest flower! It grows to nearly three feet (one meter) across the middle.

Many plants have colorful flowers and a strong smell to attract insects to them. The rafflesia has a terrible smell.

The flower appears when the plant is ready to be pollinated. It smells of rotten meat or rotten eggs. Flies love this smell and are attracted to the flower.

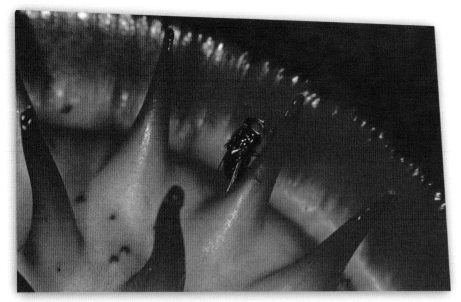

The flies crawl around the rafflesia and get covered in pollen. Then they spread the pollen from flower to flower.

**The rafflesia grows in rainforest habitats in Southeast Asia.**

**The rafflesia has no leaves or roots – just a giant flower that lives for only a few days.**

Pitcher plants come
in lots of different
shapes and colors.

# Pitcher plant

Pitcher plants grow in rainforests and places where the ground is damp. Pitcher plants are **carnivorous** plants. They attract insects that fall into the pitcher, where they are broken down and used as food.

The pitcher is like a thin tube. When insects come to taste the sweet juice inside the tube, they slide down the slippery sides and cannot get out again.

**Ant**

The insects drown in the pool of juice at the bottom of the tube. Their body is broken down and digested by the plant.

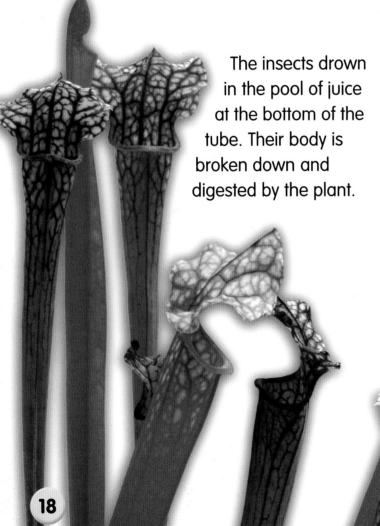

**AMAZING
PLANT FACT**

Some pitcher plants use the nutrients in snails, frogs, and even small mice as food!

The pitcher plant grows flowers in early spring, which are pollinated by bees.

The plant makes seeds inside the flowers. The seeds fall to the ground when they are **ripe**.

**Flower**

**The pitcher is part of the leaf.**

**Leaf**

**Tendril**

The pitcher is attached to the leaf by a long, thin tendril.

# Saguaro cactus

The saguaro cactus plant can live for over 200 years. When the saguaro is about 70 years old, it begins to produce flowers.

**The saguaro cactus stores water in its trunk.**

Buds appear in spring on the top of the main trunk and arms. The buds open into large white flowers.

Bats, bees, and birds feed on nectar from the flowers. They pick up pollen from the flowers on their bodies.

## AMAZING PLANT FACT

Saguaro flowers open in the middle of the night and then close up again at lunchtime the next day.

**The plant's prickles stop animals from eating it!**

When the animals carry pollen from one cactus to another, pollination happens, and the cactus produces seeds.

Gila woodpeckers make nest holes in the saguaro's trunk.

This Gila woodpecker carries pollen from cactus to cactus.

**Flower**

**Bud**

# Coconut palm

Inside a coconut is the white part, called meat, which we can eat.

Coconut palm trees have male and female flowers growing on the same tree. When the female flowers are pollinated, new seeds form. The fruits of a palm tree are called coconuts.

**AMAZING PLANT FACT**
Coconut shells can be used to make pots and cups.

The coconuts grow in bunches under the palm tree's leaves.

When the coconuts are ripe, they fall to the ground.

Young coconuts are filled with sweet liquid.

Coconut palms often grow on beaches. Many coconuts are washed out to sea. They float along until they land on another beach.

**Coconut**

**Shoot**

When the coconut reaches a new place, shoots will start to grow. This new palm tree will be ready to flower and produce seeds in about seven years.

**Eye**

Inside the skin of a coconut is a thick hairy covering. Under the covering is the seed coat, which has three pores called "eyes." The new shoot grows from one eye and the root from another.

23

# Squirting cucumber

The plant's yellow flowers are pollinated by insects such as bees.

The squirting cucumber grows on sandy or stony ground. The plant has a thick hairy stem that trails along the ground. The fruit of the plant is long and green. It looks a bit like a small hairy cucumber.

The fruit fills up with juice and seeds. It gets fatter and fatter. When the fruit is ripe, it suddenly explodes! The seeds inside are fired out like bullets.

**Fruit**

**AMAZING PLANT FACT**

The seeds of the squirting cucumber shoot out of the fruit at up to 62 miles (100 kilometers) an hour!

There are about 25 to 50 seeds in each fruit.

**Seed**

This empty fruit has dried up. You can still see some seeds stuck inside.

The squirting cucumber belongs to a group of plants called gourds. The fruits can be dried and the empty shells used to make cups, bowls, or musical instruments.

Gourd plants have fruits with a hard outer covering.

This is a gourd rattle.

# Baobab tree

Baobab trees live on hot, dry grasslands in Africa. When it rains, the tree can store up to 26,000 gallons (100,000 liters) of water in its trunk – enough to fill a backyard swimming pool!

**Baobab seeds are eaten by elephants, antelopes, and monkeys.**

The tree stays bare for nine months of the year. Then it grows leaves and flowers. The big white flowers open up during the night.

The flowers smell sweet and attract nighttime animals, such as bats. The animals get pollen on their bodies and help to pollinate the flowers. Then the tree produces big fruits.

**You can see the flower's anthers.**

**This man is holding a baobab fruit. You can see the seeds inside.**

Bats and other animals that eat baobab seeds spread them in their droppings.

The baobab is also called the upside-down tree because it looks as if its roots are growing at the top of the tree.

**AMAZING PLANT FACT**

A baobab tree starts flowering when it is about 20 years old. It can live for up to 3,000 years!

# Resurrection fern

This fern lives by attaching itself to another plant. It lives on large trees, such as oak trees. The fern gets the water and nutrients it needs from the **bark** of the tree and from the air.

**The leaves of ferns are called fronds.**

When there is no rain, the fronds of the resurrection fern turn brown, shrivel up, and look dead. The fern can live like this for years.

**AMAZING PLANT FACT**

"Resurrection" means "to come back to life." This fern gets its name because it almost dies and then comes back to life again!

After just one rain shower, the fronds uncurl, turn green, and seem to come back to life.

Ferns do not make seeds. Instead they have tiny spores that are so small you need a microscope to see them.

The spores grow on the underside of the fronds.

These brown spots are called sori. The spores are inside the sori.

Spores are carried in the wind. When a spore lands on a suitable place, it grows a very thin root called a rhizoid. This root supplies the spore with water. The spore grows into a new fern.

# That's amazing!

Plants are a necessary part of every habitat. Plants can give animals and people food and shelter. In return, animals can help plants to survive in lots of ways!

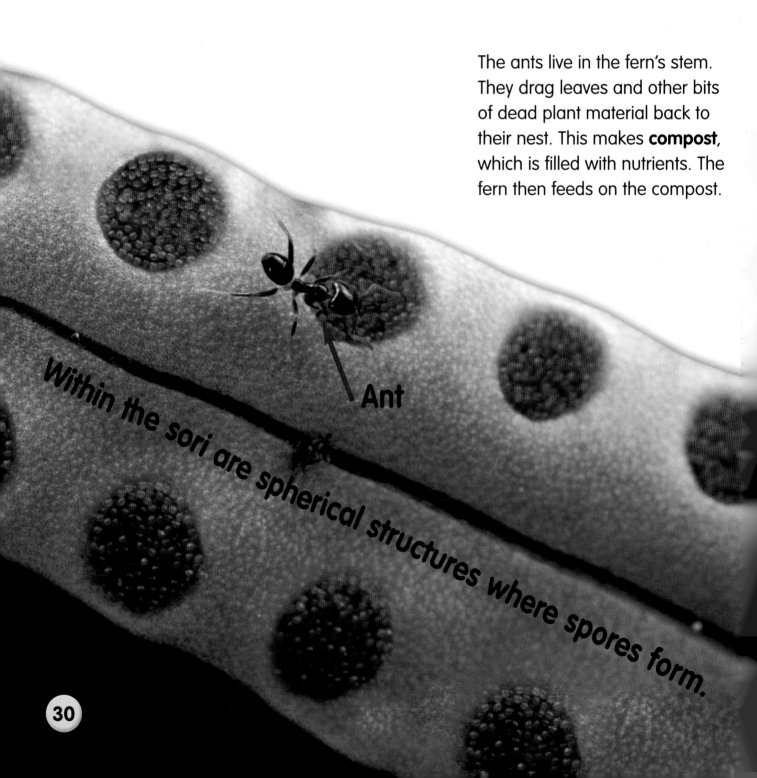

**Do you like eating these seeds?**

The ants live in the fern's stem. They drag leaves and other bits of dead plant material back to their nest. This makes **compost**, which is filled with nutrients. The fern then feeds on the compost.

Ant

Within the sori are spherical structures where spores form.

# A burr is a seed with a prickly covering.

Sometimes animals brush past plants that have burrs. The burrs get stuck in the animals' hair or fur and are carried to a new place, where the seed can grow.

**This is a burr from a burdock plant.**

Some plants have flowers that look like insects and are fertilized when males of the species try to mate with the flower.

## AMAZING PLANT FACT

The bee orchid has a flower that looks like a bee so that real bees will visit the flower and pollinate it.

# Glossary

**bark** – The outer layer of a tree's trunk.

**carnivorous** – The word to describe an animal or plant that eats meat.

**compost** – Decaying leaves and bits of plants that provide nutrients to the soil.

**desert** – A very dry place. Most deserts are very hot in the day. Some deserts get cold at night.

**fruits** – Fleshy parts grown by a plant, which contain the plant's seeds.

**nectar** – A sweet liquid inside flowers. Insects, bats, and birds drink nectar.

**nutrients** – Substances found in food that nourish animals and plants.

**pollen** – A dust produced by the anthers (male parts) of plants. Pollen is needed to make seeds.

**pollination** – When pollen is carried from the anthers of one flower to the stigma of another flower.

**rainforests** – Dense forests of tall trees in places with lots of rain.

**reproduce** – To make seeds that will grow into new plants. To have babies.

**ripe** – The time when a seed is ready to be dispersed and develop into a new plant.

**seed** – The part of a plant that can grow to become a new plant.

**soil** – The layer of dirt in which plants grow.

**stages** – Different times of a plant's life when the plant changes in some way.

# Index